# Cover Yc ⌐ ᴊ

*The true story of one woman's fight*

*to recover from severe mental illness*

## Gerry Baird

Clearstone
Publishing

# INTRODUCTION

The winter of 2016-2017 was the most difficult season I have ever experienced. I suffer from depression, which is especially active during the winter months, and had reached the lowest point in my life. Nothing was interesting to me anymore, even things I had enjoyed only weeks before. That's when I met Joan, someone whose tragic backstory makes even the worst childhood look like a day at an amusement park. As I worked tirelessly to keep Joan from ending her own life, I was amazed to discover that she was actually saving me. Joan (not her real name) was a fighter who had reached the end of her rope. A few years before I met her, she'd put a bullet in her chest and survived. She was unbelievably angry when she woke up in the hospital, because she thought she'd found the final solution, a way to end her immense pain. Joan's father was one of the most evil people ever to walk the Earth. He abused her horrifically, and it was a blessing when he died.

Outwardly, Joan was a saint. She refused to carry on her father's abuse, choosing the opposite path instead. She became a social worker, and her main motivation for helping others was not wanting them to ever feel as bad as she felt. She also studied psychology and hired a therapist in an effort to fix herself, but had been unable to do so after more than a decade of trying. Inwardly, Joan's emotional world was a shattered wasteland of seemingly irreparable psychological damage. Her self-esteem was barely extant, and she blamed herself for everything that had happened to her. Her father's abuse must have been her fault, her trauma-reasoning convinced her, otherwise why would he have done what he did?

A series of miracles began to occur almost the moment Joan and I started talking. She had completely written off God and anything related to the spiritual world, but as a religious and spiritual person myself, I gently introduced her to various tools that were quite effective. It was an intuitive process, as I had no formal training in psychology or spirituality. I was simply a friend who grew to love her, and I believe love was the key ingredient that had been missing in her life. Her father had always said, "I love you," then treated her like garbage, so she came to the conclusion that love was something to be avoided. She was a champion of kindness, however, and after several months of discussion and persuasion, I was able to help her understand that what she called kindness was actually love.

Every time I talked with Joan, which I did quite often, I learned something new. Much of what we experienced pushed the limits and boundaries of my spiritual beliefs, which I had previously felt I understood well. I quickly realized I knew very little about how God and the universe function. I also began to wonder about many of the current approaches to psychiatry and psychology. My experience with Joan made me think there is much about the causes and cures of mental illness that those professions have yet to discover.

There are still so many things I do not understand, but I know this story needs to be shared. I present the facts as I experienced them, and leave the task of explaining the unexplainable to the reader.

## MEETING JOAN

Joan and I met in a Facebook group for anxiety and depression. She asked how to overcome an addiction, and I responded that it helps to have a team that includes friends, religious leaders, therapists, and other resources to support recovery. She said, "I have no one." I volunteered to be her first team member, and told her I'd check in with her daily. My intention at the time was to fill a role similar to an Alcoholics Anonymous sponsor. I didn't know it would quickly become one of the closest friendships I've ever enjoyed.

The primary reason I was in that group was to help others. I had visited a therapist for the first time a year earlier, after experiencing a serious setback in life. She told me I'd make a good therapist. I've always been an empathetic person, sometimes overly so, and I worried that if I were to become a therapist I would find it too difficult to listen to people's problems all day. I didn't want to carry those problems home with me or take them on as if they were my own, so I decided to try an experiment. I joined an online relationship group and began giving advice to people who were struggling. At first it was difficult to read about people's challenges, especially when so many of them seemed irresolvable. However, as I began to participate I soon discovered I could not only handle the emotional content, but I actually thrived in that environment. I became quite adept at offering empathy, support and solutions.

When I was fourteen years old, I had a huge chip on my shoulder. I had a good life, but I had chosen to live at the level of anger and revenge. I had an experience the summer before I turned fifteen that changed me forever. Someone was rude to me, and I was planning to get revenge. Then the person surprised me by apologizing and extending a hand of friendship. I realized I had been about to hurt a good person, and in that moment I dedicated my life to making a positive difference. My primary motivation changed from revenge to kindness.

A few months before I began talking with Joan, I read a book called "Living Beautifully with Uncertainty and Change" by Pema Chodron. It asked a very poignant question: who is not worthy of love? I realized I had been selectively loving people, but after reading that book I wanted to learn to love everyone. An energetic shift occurred inside me, and soon random strangers began to connect with me via social media and share their deepest secrets. I responded with love and acceptance. When Joan and I started talking, I showed her that same kindness.

I didn't know it until later, but Joan was very afraid of me at first. Because of the abuse she had suffered, she was particularly afraid of males. It was a miracle she connected with me at all. She asked herself when I sent her a friend request, "How is he going to hurt me?" That's what she said whenever she had to interact with males. It was the way she'd been programmed to relate to the world. A week or two prior to us connecting, however, she had been quietly reading the group posts and made a note in her phone about me: "Where do I know him from?" I, of course, knew none of this. My only intent was to be of assistance, if I could.

# SPIRITUALITY

As a teenager, Joan spent several years in foster care. She happened to be housed with two families who attended the Church of Jesus Christ of Latter-day Saints, also known as the Mormon or LDS Church. I am a member of that church as well. One of the basic beliefs of Mormons is that the Holy Ghost or Spirit can be felt in certain situations, such as during a positive religious experience. The Church sends missionaries all over the world, and a key role the missionaries play is helping people learn about the LDS Church, read the Book of Mormon, feel the Spirit and learn for themselves, through that emotional experience, that the Church is true.

Joan, because of her severely abusive past, couldn't feel the Spirit. She couldn't feel anything. She suppressed it all. As a social worker, she regularly supervised interns who were working towards licensure. One intern was asked to inform a family about a death that had occurred. The situation was so upsetting to the intern that she decided to quit and pursue a different career. This made no sense to Joan, who was able to face such situations without batting an eye. She wasn't cold or impersonal - in fact she cared quite a lot for others, because she didn't want anyone to ever deal with the depression and pain she had experienced — but situations like that simply didn't seem difficult to her. She'd experienced far, far worse.

When Joan joined the LDS Church, it was a necessarily intellectual process. She learned about emotions by reading about them, and this approach gave her the ability to talk about emotions with clients in a helpful way, though she was limited in her ability to personally experience them. Since feeling the Spirit and experiencing emotions of joy and peace is typical prior to baptism, Joan had to get special permission from an LDS Church leader to be baptized. She was very open about the fact that she'd never felt the Holy Ghost, but two of her foster home stays were with LDS families and she appreciated the lifestyle and results associated with being LDS. It took her quite a while to join the Church, but eventually she did.

Church members often describe the experience of having the Holy Ghost come upon them as a "burning in the bosom", a warm feeling in the chest associated with happiness and love. Because of Joan's abuse, some of which involved cigarette burns on her chest, a warm feeling would have been anything but comforting.

The decision to suppress emotions had not been a conscious one. Joan wondered at times why others seemed to experience life differently. She was always looking for ways to help herself recover some semblance of psychological normalcy. She had a therapist, did electroshock therapy, and took medications. One psychiatrist recommended she try tanning regularly to help improve her mood, and she took this advice. Unfortunately, there were severely negative consequences later on as a result.

Within a few days after I started talking with Joan, she began to notice what she referred to as a "hugging feeling." I assumed this was what LDS Church members call feeling the Spirit, and I was happy she was feeling it. However, along with the hugging feeling she also began to feel ALL her feelings. Unable to cry at all for many years prior to our becoming friends, she now couldn't stop crying. She cried for three months straight. Not just quiet tears that slowly seep out of the eyes, but ugly crying that makes noise and leaves you congested and looking like you haven't slept in three days. She went through more tissues in three months than in her entire life before that.

I was surprised by her tears and the sudden appearance of her emotions. I began to talk with her about the idea of spiritual awakening, and how it is often preceded by a period referred to as the dark night of the soul. Having had several awakening experiences prior to meeting Joan, I knew it was helpful to have a guide on the journey and supported her as well as I could. My daily check-in with her quickly became several times a day, and soon we were talking for several hours each time we connected. We used Facebook messenger exclusively at the start, though we did have some phone calls later.

I had made a very difficult decision about my employment two months prior to meeting Joan. I received a job offer, then my current employer gave me a counter offer. I was torn because I had made emotional connections at my job, but I wasn't sure what direction things were going at the company. After weeks of struggle, making myself sick trying to decide what to do, I chose to keep the job I already had. This worked out perfectly for me and Joan, because due to some management decisions I ended up with a lot of downtime. I used that time to talk with Joan, who needed a friend.

The reason Joan posted on Facebook wanting advice about ending an addiction is that she had a cutting problem. Most people are very misinformed when it comes to such things. Cutting seems crazy to them, but as I talked about it with Joan I began to understand the role cutting played in her life. It wasn't just due to a masochistic desire to inflict pain on herself. It was actually the only way she knew how to cope with internal emotional trauma, and to her it was actually a pain release, not a pain increase. The endorphins that accompanied cutting calmed both her physical and her emotional discomfort.

# SCARS

When Joan was eleven years old, her father got her pregnant. He took her across state lines to get an abortion. Young, scared, and uncertain, when the nurse asked how she'd gotten pregnant, she told the truth. Joan was removed from her home and put in the foster care system. She blamed herself for being weak and telling the truth about the incest, getting her father in trouble. She also blamed herself for the abortion, feeling it was somehow her fault. Her father had deliberately programmed her to believe that if she ever told anyone about his physical and sexual abuse, he'd kill her.

The night she arrived at her foster home, she cut for the first time, carving the words "I hate life" into her ankle. She cut daily after that, utterly unable to stop herself as the emotional pain began to surface. Though she'd left her home, the abuse continued. Her father would pick her up from school, abuse her and leave her to find her way back to whatever foster home she was staying in at the time. An investigation began, but Joan was far too afraid of her father to tell the honest truth, so progress was slow. The investigator was persistent, though, gradually developing trust with Joan over a long period of time.

I never met Joan in person. It was something we both wanted, but she lived eight hours away and I think she was worried her physical appearance would detract from our friendship. She did send me a few pictures of herself, though. Once she sent me a picture of her arm, which looked like raw hamburger. Many years of cutting daily had taken their toll. She'd even cut a few tendons, limiting the mobility of some of her fingers. The cuts were all over her body.

Joan experienced a lot of judgment about her appearance. Once when she was attending church, a teen girl saw her scars and, knowing cutting was bad but knowing little of human compassion, confronted Joan about her habit. Doctors treated Joan like an object, many of them feeling their time could have been better spent helping people who were victims of unfortunate circumstances rather than self-inflicted wounds, but Joan was a victim of some of the most unfortunate circumstances imaginable.

Joan began taking medication specifically designed to increase her nerve sensitivity. By nature, she had a high tolerance for pain. Some of this may have been genetic, and some of it may have been due to being raised in an environment where pain was omnipresent. It may have simply increased her already high tolerance.

Joan's father had been a bull rider, and in one accident he'd lost both his leg and his teeth. His missing limb made it hard for him to get down in the floor, so Joan quickly learned this was the safest place she could hide. For most of her life she preferred to be on the floor with a blanket and some pillows rather than on a bed.

Joan and I began to count the number of days she went without cutting. Previously, even while in institutions or residential treatment centers, Joan had never gone 24 hours without cutting. The combination of talking to me and the nerve-sensitivity medication helped her achieve feats she never had before. She made it six days, then twelve. Each relapse was frustrating for her, but I regularly reminded her she was making great progress and doing more than she'd ever done before to help end her addiction. I assured her that it was safe to tell me about any relapses, and encouraged her to go to the hospital for stitches whenever she did cut. Joan's therapist recommended that she keep razor blades on hand, which seemed like a strange suggestion, but it kept Joan from using a kitchen knife, which would have caused much more damage.

Joan struggled with authority figures of any kind, and doctors triggered her quite severely. She was in a downward spiral of cutting, feeling ashamed, needing stitches, having a miserable experience at the doctor's office, then wanting to cut again in order to cope with both the negativity of the experience and her negative emotions that were still present from childhood. While she was at the doctor's office, I would endeavor to talk her through the difficult experience. I tried a variety of strategies, but inevitably Joan would descend into an almost primal mode at some point, becoming her wounded inner child. Usually our conversation would devolve into me giving her short instructions like "breathe in" and "breathe out." I reassured her it would be done soon and told her she was okay, everything was okay. I think it helped her to have my words to focus on in addition to what was happening around her.

Joan's father was from Germany. His parents were Nazi's, and after his father died his mother married another Nazi. He and his brother came to America when he was nineteen. After arriving in their new country, they made it as far west as they could, stopping only when they ran out of money. I asked Joan once if her father was sociopathic or insane. I trusted her opinion on this, since she knew him better than anyone else, and had studied psychology so extensively. She said he was cold and calculating and fully accountable for his hurtful choices. In all her work with the mentally ill, she never encountered someone like him.

# MENTAL HEALTH

One of the most important decisions I made along the way, and it came very naturally, was to take Joan entirely at face value. I can't say this would be the right approach in every case, but I felt strongly that Joan wasn't crazy, even when she told me an evil voice had been her constant companion for many years. We all have "voices" in our minds, little whispers and temptations that invite us to do or not do certain things. This isn't what Joan meant when she told me about her voice. It was a literal voice that sometimes screamed at her. It would tell her to cut or kill herself, and try to convince her the world wasn't a safe place. After many years of fruitless study and struggle, she began to lose all hope in her ability to heal.

There are few stones Joan left unturned in an effort to fix herself. She earned her master's in social work and even got halfway through a Ph.D. program. Instead of choosing the easiest classes, she picked the ones she felt would help her learn the most. She read every book about human behavior she could get her hands on. She was a walking encyclopedia who could correctly make very difficult diagnoses after spending a short period of time with clients. I began to talk with Joan about some of the challenging people in my life, and she explained the underlying reasons for their behavior. It opened my eyes, and I began to see the world in a whole new way.

A year before meeting Joan, I had been fired from my job. It was a very difficult experience that caused me to doubt myself and feel ashamed. I'd never been fired before, but had found myself in a bad situation. My anxiety and depression took over, making things even worse. I was completely burned out, and Joan began talking to me about the importance of self-care. I was working two jobs to try to make ends meet, and facing bankruptcy. There were a lot of pressures in my life, and I was buckling under the weight of them. Joan patiently reminded me that it's healthy to acknowledge my own needs and take time for myself. She encouraged me to do things for myself, like long boarding, reading, going to the music store or lying in my hammock in the back yard. It was strange at first. I felt so selfish doing those things, but for most of my life I'd been taught to think only of the needs of others. The net effect was that I ignored my own needs, and it took its toll. With Joan's help, I started feeling hopeful again.

Joan was in and out of institutions and psychiatric hospitals at various times throughout her life. They were extremely difficult places to be, and there were some humiliating and horrific experiences. Antipsychotics suppressed her negative voice, but also made her feel like a zombie. Institutions use chemical restraints to control patients, so Joan learned to fight the sedatives. With enough anger, they couldn't have their intended effect. She refused to be controlled.

Joan dealt with nightmares and flashbacks, the effects of post-traumatic stress disorder (PTSD). She hadn't had a good night's sleep in decades. Flashbacks would often come as a result of the nightmares, and remain with her throughout the day. She rarely got a break. The flashbacks were so intense it was as if she were being abused all over again. It wasn't just a memory; it was real to her, something she could tangibly feel in her body. She had no power over the nightmares or body memories, and I wanted to help but wasn't sure how.

For several years, Joan did electroshock therapy. The idea behind this treatment approach is that it makes patients experience a brief seizure, changing brain chemistry and relieving the symptoms of some mental illnesses. It results in memory loss. Joan was hoping to forget her traumatic experiences, but unfortunately those remained and she forgot positive ones, such as her graduation. She finally stopped electroshock therapy when she went to a psychiatrist who told her that it works well for those suffering from depression that isn't trauma-induced.

## EARLY EXPERIENCES

When Joan was in first grade, a student trying to write "six" accidentally wrote "sex". The teacher was upset, explaining to all the children that "sex" was bad and they shouldn't write that word. Joan felt very ashamed, because none of the other kids knew what sex was, but she did. Another time, the teacher wrote the word "God" on the board. Joan pointed out that she'd spelled "good" wrong, and the teacher explained that she wrote the word she had intended to write. Joan had never even heard of God, having grown up being taught that this life is all there is.

There were no interior doors in Joan's home, and because she was never allowed to visit the houses of friends and classmates, she didn't know this wasn't normal. Joan's father once set fire to the house, resulting in some burns for all inside, because he thought one of the kids had told about the abuse.

# INVESTIGATION

While in foster care, Joan's psychological issues became evident, and there was talk about putting her in a mental institution. The idea of going to an institution scared her so much that she decided to run away. Not knowing where else to go, she ended up at her father's house. He immediately began abusing her even worse than before. Afterward, Joan called the investigator who came to pick her up. Joan decided to tell her everything, and there was enough evidence to arrest Joan's father. He pleaded insanity and was sent to the same institution where Joan had been only a month earlier. While there, he committed suicide. Though he was gone, the effects of his abuse remained. Even later in life, it was an immense struggle for Joan to say anything about her early experiences. The brainwashing her father had subjected her to remained intact and effective, making it difficult for her to heal. Rather than rejoicing, she blamed herself for causing her father's death.

# COUNSELING

Within a week or two after Joan and I started talking, she told me about a simple change model involving three stages: contemplation, preparation and execution. I realized that when it came to changing careers, I had been bouncing between contemplation and preparation but never actually taken the first step towards licensure. My challenge was that I couldn't see how to overcome a couple of obstacles. First, I wasn't sure how I would find the time for the required practicum/internship experience at the end of the program, and second I wasn't sure I could afford the pay cut switching to counseling would involve. I wanted meaningful work, though, and after seeing what Joan could do with her knowledge of human behavior, I decided I would start on the path and see where it led. I enrolled in an online counseling program and slowly began working towards my goal.

# MUSIC

Music had always been Joan's passion, and her escape from an insanely difficult life. She was a naturally gifted musician who eventually become a drum major in high school. She did this without being able to read a single note. Her high school band teacher encouraged her to learn to read notes, so she did. She was able to earn a scholarship and got a degree in music teaching. Her whole house was filled with musical instruments. As far as I could tell, there wasn't an instrument she couldn't play. Her favorite was tuba. She participated in the tuba Christmas concert every year. She even went to Germany and bought her tuba custom-made from the factory, placing the final valves on the instrument herself. She told me if she ever sold her tuba, I should be worried because it probably meant she was thinking of ending her life soon.

# RELATIONSHIPS

Not surprisingly, Joan struggled with relationships. She dated two men who were very much like her father. She felt it was what she deserved. One of them broke her eye socket. Another held his hand over her mouth when she had the vomiting flu because he didn't want her to throw up. She ended up chocking down her vomit, which could have killed her had it entered her lungs. After these abusive experiences, Joan decided to always have a credit card and an overnight bag in her car in case she needed to leave in a hurry.

Her father told her once, "You're so broken, the only one who will ever love you is me." It was an interesting comment from a man who had no idea what love even is. Fortunately, he was wrong. Joan did find somebody who loved her, and he was quite wonderful. I'll call him Henry. The relationship began when Joan was a music teacher, and Henry showed up to a junior high school band concert to support Joan. She knew then that it was true love, because no one would voluntarily show up for a junior high music concert except to see their own child perform.

Henry was a good, kind man. He was gentle with Joan, and there was a part of her that resented him for it. She told me it made her sick. She didn't feel she deserved his love or kindness, but she dated him for three years and agreed to marry him. She was nervous about her ability to be married, due to her history of abuse, but for his sake she wanted to try. A few days before the wedding, while they were kissing, something he did triggered a memory of her father and she immediately ran out of the apartment, not stopping until she was in the next city, 25 miles away. She called off the wedding, but she never stopped loving Henry. He moved on out of necessity, never fully understanding what he'd done wrong. He became a therapist in an effort to better understand her, and the two of them remained in touch over the years.

## THE LICENSING BOARD

There is a licensing board in each state that is responsible for regulating the practice of counseling and social work. Its primary responsibility is to protect clients from harmful counseling practices, and they also ensure that professional codes of ethics are followed. An example of an ethical violation that could cause a counselor's license to be revoked is a therapist having a sexual relationship with a current client. The licensing board also wants to make sure that counselors are competent to practice, and not causing harm to clients.

Joan's mental health history and periodic psychiatric hospital stays were very concerning to the licensing board. In most cases, a counselor with several emotional issues would struggle to effectively guide clients. This wasn't the case with Joan, though the licensing board didn't understand why. Despite her many psychological challenges, no one had ever filed a complaint against her. Still, the licensing board got involved when she was unable to stop cutting, putting limits on her license and requiring her to see a therapist. Every few months she needed to meet with them, and it was after her most difficult meeting, during which they threatened to take her license if something didn't change in three months, that she made her desperate post on the Facebook group that brought us together.

# FOOD

There is a connection between sexual abuse and weight. Some women consciously or subconsciously put on weight in order to feel more confident in their ability to fend off attackers or be less attractive to them and therefore less vulnerable to attack. Joan, due to her father's preferences, had the opposite response. It was always a struggle for her to eat. Even though her father had passed away, her traumatized brain felt safer from him when she was unhealthily thin. When her emotions returned full-force a few days after we started talking, her eating habits rapidly began to decline. Since we never met in person, I was unaware of the issue until she mentioned it. Between her crying and rapid weight loss, people were getting concerned.

Joan had quite a remarkable gift for reaching those no one else seemed to care about or know how to handle. One was a man named Mark who had Down Syndrome. He'd been in an abusive situation, and when he first came to the clinic where Joan worked he didn't say a word. In fact, at their first meeting he hit Joan, then felt sorry about it. Slowly Mark began to open up to her. She reached him through kindness and music, dancing in her office to his favorite band Kiss.

She treated him the way she would treat any other person, and he helped her learn that hugs can be positive. During her childhood, hugs had always led to something more and were therefore to be feared.

When Mark saw how quickly Joan was losing weight, he asked her if she was going to die soon. His words stung, and she wondered if he was right.

# DISABILITY

While Joan was working as a social worker at a hospital, some friends encouraged her to apply for disability. She didn't want to do it, but because they pressured her she decided to appease them. Typically, it takes a year or two and a lot of effort to be approved, but Joan was approved instantly. It left her wondering how mentally ill she really was. Part of the reason her application was accepted so readily is that in her efforts to help herself, she'd never missed a therapy appointment. To the government, it appeared that Joan was willing to do whatever it took to get better, and they rewarded her efforts by granting disability pay. She didn't take advantage of it until later, when she was no longer able to work.

Work was a source of pride for Joan. She wanted to make a contribution. Her role as a therapist was so meaningful to her that it became part of her identity. She was almost insulted that the government approved her disability request so easily, indicating to her that she wasn't cut out to contribute as a full member of society.

# KINDNESS

Joan worried that in spite of her best efforts, she still had her father's DNA in her and was therefore a monster like him. Her negative voice supported that hypothesis, though she was as far removed from his personality as she could possibly be. Where he'd been awful, she

15

was kind. Where he'd been selfish, she was selfless. She told me that during her therapy sessions with clients, the dark, scared, sad part of herself would hide in the proverbial corner and her light and love and skill would take over. That's why no client ever filed a complaint against her, because she was very good at her job.

I found that it was difficult to compliment Joan. Almost immediately I saw that she was good and kind, but had simply been dealt a bad hand. When she would tell me about kind things she had done for others, I would point them out, but she would dismiss them, saying it was just "what anyone else would do." One day, Joan was at the store and ran into someone who recognized her. Unfortunately, she had no memory of the other person due to her electroshock therapy. He reminded her that she had been the first on the scene of their car accident a few years before. She had made sure he and his wife were okay before running to catch their dog, who had escaped from the car after the accident and was wandering scared on the side of the highway. When she shared this story with me, she told me that's the kind of heroism that qualifies as kindness. The everyday, normal stuff she regularly did for people didn't count. We agreed to disagree.

# LOVE

Love was a very difficult topic for Joan. She had a nephew who was her pride and joy. He called her daily and told her he loved her. She could never bring herself to say it back. Although very unusual for me in any context except a romantic relationship, I felt early on that I needed to tell Joan I loved her. I saw the good in her that she couldn't see, and I wanted to express that somehow. At first it literally hurt her to see those words on her screen, and she couldn't write them back to me. I said it sparingly in the beginning, looking for moments when she might be able to actually receive the message. I asked, after a while, if she wanted me to stop staying it. She said no, although it still hurt. She wanted to learn to be okay with the idea of love. Eventually, as she saw that my actions lined up with my words, she began to accept the idea of love and soon was saying it back to both me and to her nephew when he said it.

# VISUALIZATIONS

When Joan's negative voice took over, it was very difficult to reach her. I was quite impressed that she was able to still talk to me even when the voice was screaming at her to ignore me. We decided to name the voice Fred, just so we could personify it enough to separate it from herself. She had an idea one time to try putting Fred in a box, just to see if we would be able to quiet it. The experiment worked, and for a few days she had peace. It was the first time in years her negative voice had been quiet. The voice still came back often, sometimes for no apparent reason and sometimes because she began to feel afraid or suicidal, but we were able to take care of it each time through the use of visualizations. The process would take ten or twenty minutes from start to finish. We'd begin by digging a hole, then we'd run around and gather up Fred – symbolized by a gelatinous red blob – and toss it into the hole. Then we'd back up a cement truck and pour it over the top.

The visualizations began to vary over time. Sometimes Joan wanted to put Fred in a prison cell lined with razors and knives and glass, or even fire. The violence was uncomfortable for me, but since Fred was basically her abuser, I decided it was at least commensurate with what she'd suffered and went along with it. This was her visualization, after all, so we did it her way. We drowned Fred, buried Fred in quicksand, put Fred on an airplane and sent it off to who knows where (Fred wasn't even worthy of having a gender). When the visualizations became less violent, I asked Joan why and she said she didn't have the energy for it.

We found two quicker techniques for containing Fred in emergency situations, when Joan was in danger of hurting herself and Fred needed to be immediately silenced. One was to picture Fred being sucked out of her head and into a vacuum, then deposited in the garbage. This silenced Fred, as well as removing any accompanying body memories. The other technique involved casting out demons in the name of Christ, following Biblical methods. Joan was open to all options as long as they were effective.

# THE HAMMOCK

Another helpful visualization Joan and I created together was a hammock in a meadow. It was a mental happy place where she could escape her suffering for a while. A safe place was essential for Joan, since so much of her world was or appeared to be extremely dangerous. Creating the hammock took several hours the first time, as Joan was in a very negative state and it was hard for her to even picture what peace and happiness looked like. Fred showed up in his red blob form, this time with spikes, and we had to beat it back with swords. Once we'd established a foothold, however, the hammock became our go-to visualization. All of this was very metaphorical and guided by Joan, with me as an observer and companion. Slowly, the hammock area grew into quite a beautiful place. There was a pond with ducks, a meadow, and roses with no thorns so Joan wasn't tempted to cut herself. There was a caterpillar that over a period of weeks crawled into a cocoon and became a butterfly as Joan began to heal.

The weather in the hammock area could vary depending on Joan's mood. Sometimes it was cloudy and gray, other times blue and sunny. It rained occasionally, usually when Joan felt like crying, and a few times there was even a rainbow. Birds occasionally sang, and scents sometimes wafted over Joan. Occasionally we invited Jesus to join us there, and once her nephew came and skipped rocks in the pond.

# JOB LOSS

Joan began reporting her weight to me regularly when it became clear that something was very wrong. She loved to run long distances, which caused the weight loss to accelerate. I also found out later that she was taking diuretics and laxatives because she felt she was too fat, even after losing more than 50% of her body weight in a matter of weeks. Her therapist diagnosed her with anorexia, which was a difficult label for Joan to accept. She was a cornucopia of diagnoses, but I stayed focused on the person beneath the label. Between the rapid weight loss and constant crying, Joan's boss began to be very concerned about her. He slowly began reducing her client load, eventually leaving her with only one day of work each week. This devastated her emotionally and financially. Her boss was male, which didn't help, and she saw him as the enemy. After a lot of soul searching, Joan decided to quit her job and go on disability pay.

# SUICIDE

It was a lot of work to keep Joan from ending her life. She saw it as the only way to escape her pain, since healing seemed to be an absolute impossibility. We made a lot of safety plans and agreements and contracts along the way. One time I talked her out of ending her life simply because no one would be there to contact me and let me know what had happened. Although in great pain herself, she had no desire to cause pain for others. She told me that when she shot herself a few years before, she felt perfect peace before pulling the trigger. She believed it was because she'd finally made a clear decision and was no longer wrestling with what to do. When Joan quit her job, she lost a part of her identity, and she once more was contemplating suicide since she no longer had a sense of purpose. I encouraged her to pawn her gun so it wouldn't tempt her. She listened, and even asked if there was a list she could put her name on that would keep her from being able to buy a gun in the future if she became suicidal again. There wasn't. I think for those who struggle with suicidal tendencies, a voluntary list like that could be an excellent amendment to state law.

After her failed attempt a few years before, Joan was found by a neighbor who heard the gunshot. The neighbor's quick action saved Joan's life. Years later, when Joan was feeling upset one day, she put on some loud music and the same neighbor, worrying Joan was trying to cover up a gunshot, came over to make sure she was okay. While Joan and I were talking, this neighbor asked Joan to take care of her cats. Unfortunately, she didn't think to lock up her guns while she was on vacation. Every day she went over there, Joan was tempted to pick up a gun and end her life. It took all the strength and skill I had to prevent her from doing it.

Joan was obsessed with being more thorough the next time she attempted suicide, so she would be sure not to wake up. A lot of her time was spent researching effective suicide methods, and we often included prohibitions against such research activities in her safety contracts. It took all my negotiating skills to get her to agree to stop working towards suicide, and even then she would leave herself a loophole or two. There were so many times when I reached out to her at just the right time, as she prepared to go running or cut. Other times I missed the opportunity and ended up calming her while she visited the doctor to get stitches.

When I asked Joan if she had a support team and she told me she had no one, I think she was honestly reporting how she felt. As I talked with her, however, I began to see that she did have some supporters. One of these was a foster sister from her teen years I'll call Stephanie. The two of them had remained friends for many years, in spite of an incident that occurred when Stephanie pressed Joan for details about her abuse and Joan instinctually responded with physical violence. Stephanie was often the person who Joan called when she was feeling suicidal. She also checked in regularly with Joan to make sure she was okay.

# LEARNING

In what was admittedly one of the worst mistakes I made while helping Joan, one night I encouraged her to "get angry" and walk straight into her emotional pain. In my defense, it was early enough in the process that I didn't know what we were facing. She followed my advice. It led to her screaming, then hitting the wall, and she ended up breaking her hand. I felt awful, and that incident may have been one of my main motivations for going to school. I didn't want to make any more mistakes like that. Joan went out of her way to make sure I knew she didn't think I was at fault for her broken hand. After that, I decided a better approach than walking straight into her pain was to tiptoe around it, quietly softening it from the edges.

# WHITE LIGHT

Two years before I began talking with Joan, I had a remarkable dream. I was talking with Jesus, who asked me if I wanted the gift of healing. I said yes, and he put his hands on my back and filled me with white light. At the time, I didn't know what to think of the dream, or even what it meant. Did the gift of healing mean that I would be or had been healed? Was it something I could use to heal others? I had no idea.

One day while talking with Joan on the telephone about a body memory that wouldn't go away, I noticed my hands starting to tingle. I told Joan about my dream, and asked if she'd be willing to try something a little (or a lot) crazy. She agreed, and I asked her to picture my hands on her back and being filled with white light. She did as instructed. Not only did it stop the body memory, but she said she felt actual hands on her back while it was happening. It would be easy to dismiss this as the musings of a desperate and overly vivid imagination, but after having dozens of experiences like that with Joan I realized my spiritual views were very limited, and even wrong in some cases. I had learned about God in church, but the God I discovered while working with Joan was more generous, more powerful and more loving than anything I'd previously conceived. My mind couldn't process it, so my faith had to take over. Joan and I continued to use white light to help her heal. Sometimes it did very little, but other times it did what nothing else could do. It eased her pain and replaced her fear with love. It comforted her and changed her despair into joy.

# JOY

I was ecstatic the day Joan told me she had begun to hear a positive, loving female voice. We named her Joy, and I believed it was her guardian angel speaking. Joy began helping us with Fred, offering good advice to Joan and making her feel loved. Each time I sent white light, Joan would close her eyes and Joy would kiss her on the forehead. When Joan had difficult decisions to make, Joy would help. She would even wipe Joan's tears.

My assumption that what Joan described as a "hugging feeling" was the Holy Ghost turned out to be incorrect. As we discussed the details later, she was feeling a literal hug, with arms around her and a head pressed to her chest. We came to the conclusion that it was her second guardian angel, her aborted baby. We called him Gideon.

I realize both Joan and I probably appear quite delusional. From a psychological point of view, we certainly are. However, we come from a religious tradition that believes in some of the things we experienced, at least conceptually, so from a spiritual point of view we don't feel quite as crazy as one might suppose.

The New Testament describes many instances when Christ and his followers cast out demons. It isn't talked about much about these days, but I've long held the belief that those we call mentally ill may in fact simply have a greater sensitivity to the spirit world, and can sometimes be attacked by dark spirits. After seeing the miracles in Joan's life, I am also convinced that the great suffering she experienced early in life contributed to her becoming more enlightened as time went by. Because she'd seen and felt some of the worst things this world can offer, she had developed a capacity to experience some of the best. I don't know how or why the techniques we used worked. I just know that they did. Joan and I developed a strong bond through this process, and I believe the combination of love and spirituality, along with the psychological knowledge she already possessed, were the keys to her healing.

# SURRENDER

Joan had many triggers that could quickly send her into a state of panic. One of these was any use of the word "father," which unfortunately was quite common in a religious setting. Another trigger was when comments were made about her scars. She could go from content to suicidal in an instant when this kind of talk occurred. She also really struggled with the idea of surrender. Although I didn't realize it at first, Joan saw surrender as allowing an abuser to have his way with you, or giving yourself up to the police. I was thinking of surrender in a spiritual sense, as in releasing painful baggage that limits emotional progress. In her worst moments, she didn't want to trust anything or anyone, including God. She wanted complete control over her environment, and I believe her need for a level of total control that couldn't be obtained led to a lot of pain and fear. One day I sent her the song "Thy Will" by Hillary Scott, and within 30 seconds it triggered Joan's negative voice. This was something that happened periodically, and I had to be prepared for it at any given time. In this particular instance, the trigger led to a beautiful conversation about surrender that put Joan into a more positive state than she'd ever experienced before. She told me that for the first time in her life, she wanted to live.

Joan was so excited to begin her new life. She was thinking about getting a dog. She loved golden retrievers, and had had one in the past, but it was something she'd hesitated to do in recent years because she didn't want her dog to be left alone if she decided to end her life. A dog represented an investment in her future. She was thinking about driving to where I lived, visiting me and looking at some dogs being sold by a family near my home.

## MEDICAL PROBLEMS

Around this time, Joan went to the doctor to get some stitches removed. It was supposed to be a routine visit, but she passed out. I assumed her weakness was due to being severely underweight. She was taken to a hospital where tests were run, and tumors were discovered in her lungs. She'd been diagnosed with skin cancer several years before, a side-effect of her many years of doctor-recommended tanning. The cancer had been removed, but it had come back and metastasized in her lungs. It made breathing very difficult, and she was in ICU with a ventilator for a time.

I was devastated by the news. She had finally decided to live, and then she was diagnosed with cancer. The bitter irony was a difficult blow, but I am grateful the news didn't come a week earlier, when she would have treatment, seeing cancer as simply an acceptable form of suicide. Instead, Joan hoped for a full recovery and began the difficult and painful treatment process.

## HOSPITAL

Joan hated being in the hospital. For one thing, she wasn't allowed to sleep on the floor as she'd been accustomed to doing all her life. For another, hospital protocol required her to have a 24x7 sitter because of her history of self-harm and mental illness. This made Joan feel like a second-class citizen, but she tried to look at the positives, a skill we were both working to improve. She decided that it was helpful when she had a problem for someone to be right there in the room with her.

Radiation treatments were very painful. There was a "stop" button in the machine, and sometimes Joan had to hit it because she just couldn't handle it anymore. When chemotherapy started, Joan began vomiting quite often. Her skin was sensitive because of the radiation treatments, and when she vomited the chemotherapy chemicals in her system would burn it.

After a week or two at the hospital, Joan's kidneys began to fail. Her body filled with fluid and her weight doubled in a very short time. Her skin was swollen, and the discomfort was extreme. Fortunately, her doctors were able to resolve the problem and the excess water began to disappear. Painful sores from the stretching remained, however, and Joan's dressings had to be changed regularly. This was a difficult process, as it involved touching areas that triggered memories of abuse. It took four staff members to hold her down, and sometimes she had to be sedated. However, with a combination of white light and messaging with her, I was able to keep her calm enough to make it through without those extra restraints.

Joan needed surgery at one point, and went under general anesthesia for the process. While she was under, she had a near-death experience. She remembered talking to Jesus and being given the option to stay in heaven or come back. She chose to come back in order to help me through some of my life challenges. She was one of the kindest people I've ever known, and if anyone was hurting anywhere then she would willingly sacrifice her own comfort in order to help.

Fred, Joan's negative voice, sometimes took over and encouraged Joan to do harmful things. She would rip out her IVs and attempt to walk to the door. One time she broke her ankle while doing this, because her bones were so brittle from malnourishment.

When Joan's cancer began to spread, she started losing the ability to see out of one eye. This made it hard to write to me on her phone, so one night she enlisted the help of her sitter, a nurse named Gloria. When Joan fell asleep, Gloria and I continued talking. Gloria told me that Joan was a favorite patient among the hospital staff. They would spend their breaks in her room, just to be near her. Joan ended up staying in the hospital for three months.

## JOAN'S MOM

Joan's mom had left her dad when Joan was five years old. She didn't come back into Joan's life until Joan was an adult. When Joan's nephew was born, neither parent was able to raise the baby, so Joan's mom agreed to take on the task. When Joan woke up in the hospital after her suicide attempt, her mom arranged for the most important people in Joan's life to talk her through the anger she was feeling. When Joan was diagnosed with cancer, her mom immediately retired and moved to the city where Joan lived. She became her advocate, working with the legal system to prevent the hospital from using excessive sedatives in their attempts to keep Joan from hurting herself. She designated a room in her new house where Joan could stay when she was released from the hospital. Joan and I both acknowledged with immense gratitude the role her mother played in the process. Joan's mom was arguably the most important person on her support team.

## COMPLICATIONS

Several different types of chemotherapy were attempted to help Joan, but none of them worked. Either the side-effects were unmanageable, or the medicine was ineffective at reducing the size of her tumors and stopping the spread of cancer. Unfortunately, the cancer spread to her brain and lymph nodes. She began having seizures and was given medication to prevent them, which for some reason made Joan suicidal. Antidepressants helped compensate for this side-effect, but the seizure medications took effect instantly whereas the antidepressants took a few days, so each time the anti-seizure medications were increased there was a period of a few days where Joan felt life wasn't worth living. After leaving the hospital,

Joan ordered a gun during one of these episodes. In a show of great courage and trust, she confessed this and we were able to work with her mom and therapist to keep the gun from getting into her hands. Chemotherapy killed the platelets in her blood, making her susceptible to severe and life-threatening nosebleeds. Joan was regularly given units of whole blood and platelets. Although a regular blood donor, I had never before understood the amount of blood a single patient can require. Interestingly, Joan began having nosebleeds each time we cast out demons, so this practice had to stop. Also, with too many pain medications, Joan could no longer differentiate between the good and bad voices in her head. She would tell me what they said and I would report to her which voice had said it, based on the content of the message.

When Joan's nephew asked her oncologist when Joan was going to die, he replied that she continued to surprise everyone.

# FIGHTING A LOSING BATTLE

Joan was wheeled into emergency surgery to remove a growing brain tumor that was causing her seizures. After that, Joan's ability to speak, write, read and understand words was severely impaired. Her brain remained fully functional, but the language interface was impacted. It was extremely frustrating for her. Genders, numbers, dates and times were very difficult. Unable to say "Christmas" at first, she referred to it as "Jesus party day."

After trying every option, including an experimental chemotherapy treatment, the doctors came to the conclusion that there was nothing more they could do for her. As a last resort, Joan's mom applied at a major cancer center in another state, but Joan was denied because of her poor mental health history.

Joan was grateful to leave the hospital. She had begun talking to Jesus regularly, and the enlightened insights she shared with me were astounding. One day she said she wanted to hug me. "Ask Jesus hug Joan," she told me, so I did. I can only describe the warmth that followed as one of the most real sensations I'd ever experienced. Joan was hurt and scared when we first met, but somewhere along the way she became one of the most loving people I have ever known. Often she would start a conversation with me by saying something like, "Jesus talk I need talk I love you much."

## A WONDERFUL SURPRISE

One day I was walking to my car when I read an email message that Joan had written several months before and scheduled for future delivery. Tears began to stream down my face as I realized how much I missed her ability to speak in full sentences. This was her message: "Finding peace has been one of my life goals. I remember being 8 or 9 years old sitting on the edge of the loft of the barn. My father had finished having sex with me and left me there. The barn doors were open and the sun was starting to set. It was a beautiful sunset, many colors in the sky. I saw what I thought was a person in the clouds. I watched the shape change as the sun went down. It looked like the person went from angry to peaceful. Since then I have wanted to have something like the peace I imagined the cloud person having. I have found it. I hope you have found it as well. Peace is so important to our physical and emotional health."

She mentioned in the same message that she had scheduled emails to be sent to me throughout the entire next year. As Joan was on her deathbed at the time, this was an especially welcome gift.

## LEGACY

My friendship with Joan was one of the most beautiful experiences of my life. I have never been so closely connected to someone I've never met. My original intention was simply to be a positive influence on her, but it quickly became unclear who was helping whom. Both our lives were completely transformed by our friendship. I said goodbye to Joan at least a hundred times, since I never knew if it would be our last conversation. My experience with Joan is proof that love can heal and transform lives. While I am sad she got cancer, I am grateful it was natural causes and not suicide that took her from this world. Her last thoughts were of her nephew, her mom, and me, the three people she cared about most in the world. I will never forget her, and as a counselor I will endeavor to carry on her legacy of kindness.

# ABOUT THE AUTHOR

Gerry Baird is a counseling student at Grand Canyon University. He is a self-help junkie and enjoys kayaking and long boarding in his spare time. He lives in Utah, United States, and has three wonderful children.

Printed in Great Britain
by Amazon